The Mustard Seed Way

The Mustard Seed Way

Katrina Mayer

Writer's Showcase
presented by *Writer's Digest*
San Jose New York Lincoln Shanghai

The Mustard Seed Way
All Rights Reserved. © 2000 by Katrina Mayer

Published by Writer's Showcase
presented by *Writer's Digest*
an imprint of iUniverse.com, Inc.

For information address:
iUniverse.com, Inc.
620 North 48th Street
Suite 201
Lincoln, NE 68504-3467
www.iuniverse.com

ISBN: 0-595-14319-9

Printed in the United States of America

Dedication

I thank the Creator who gave me the faith and vision to bring this message to the world.

"...for verily I say unto you, if ye have faith as a grain of mustard seed, ye shall say unto this mountain, remove hence to yonder place; and it shall remove; and nothing shall be impossible unto you."

Matthew 17:20

Contents

Acknowledgements

Whenever you undertake a project of any magnitude, you realize how many people play a part in bringing it to fruition. Often there are tangible roles with names and faces. But when you sit a moment and think about it, there are hundreds, if not thousands, of people who make any particular event possible.

Since it would be difficult at best to name all those people here, I would like to thank a few who have been most supportive during the process of writing this book. My deep and heartfelt gratitude goes out to the following people:

To my Mom and Dad who always said I could be anything I wanted to be and were the first to read my book.

To my brother Eric whose pursuit of his passion inspired me to pursue mine.

To Ben, who appeared when things were at their worst and reminded me to believe.

To my friends at Barnes & Noble who entertained, amused and enlightened me many, many days and nights during the writing of this book.

To an incredible group of friends who have been a constant source of unconditional love, support and cups of tea.

To all the DJ's who "just happened" to play the songs I needed to hear, the authors who wrote the words I needed to read and the strangers who spoke truths I needed to know.

To Dr. Goldman for his undying dedication to his profession.

Introduction

Just as one might gather flowers along a path or shells on the beach, I have lovingly and joyfully gathered a collection of thoughts and feelings along my way. They were found in the shape of poems, prayers, meditations and short stories put together as I walked, ran and often stumbled along the path of life. Each serves as a remembrance of the journey, and isn't that where true joy lays–the journey itself. Along with its straight-aways and hairpin turns we often encounter a few potholes. But, have you noticed the magnificent scenery? Sometimes it is hard to see because we are rushing by so fast. But maybe, just maybe we can slow down long enough to cherish and savor the moment.

While this collection uses spiritual overtones and language, it has little to do with religion and everything to do with finding a place deep inside every living being. Or is it outside? Maybe it is both. It really makes no difference how we feel it or where we feel it. It also doesn't matter what we call it. The important point is to know that a greater good exists. This knowledge will lead us on the road to healing, both individually and collectively.

My journey has brought me through tremendous joys and also great pains, but I emphasize here that the message is not in the pain. The message is in the healing. The message has always been in the resurrection, not in the crucifixion. We can all choose to live again. We can all pull ourselves out of our self-pity, our hurts, our hells, and choose again. That is where the journey begins, and that is also when the miracles begin. So choose now, choose happily, courageously and whole-heartedly, and most of all, enjoy the journey.

Chapter 1

Begin The Journey

"The ultimate source of pain is saying that you can't do it."
The Dalai Lama, Central Park 1999

****

Bottom, as in rock bottom. You never realize exactly how hard it is until you hit it. And it hurts in ways that you never realized that you could hurt. Looking back on it I can only make one recommendation. Try it. Honestly. It is probably one of the best things that could have happened to me. And in the long run it may be one of the best things that ever happened to you, too.

I am definitely not a masochist, although you may doubt that after my last statements. But I can tell you that the experience of feeling utterly hopeless and helpless brings you to a place where you are more willing to open your heart and mind to avenues you didn't know existed. When we hit little bumps in the road, we can usually stay on it, even if the ride is uncomfortable. When we hit rock bottom, it means that the road we were on is closed. We can't go any further in that direction. Dead end. There were probably 200 detour signs that we ignored along the way. But now we reached the place where we can honestly say we don't know where to go. Congratulations.

It is not mandatory to hit rock bottom before we change our lives, however if we are there, it is possible that we can make some serious progress. We can realize just how incorrect our directions were and how badly our

1

compass malfunctioned. In many cases our judgment was poor, and we are finally willing to ask for directions. It is time to humble ourselves and search for other answers. I know that it was at this point in my life that I threw myself down on my knees and asked for help. My way hadn't worked at all. As a matter of fact, it was my best thinking that had gotten me to that point. I was willing to believe that there was another way that I was unaware of. I was willing to wait for an answer.

I had never been this desperate before. Previously I had had little catastrophes. They were nothing that I couldn't get myself out of. I was strong. I had a good head on my shoulders. I was independent. And probably worst of all, I was proud. All of these characteristics had led me to make several U-turns in my life. But somehow I kept going down the same road. No matter how many times I thought I was heading in a new direction I kept ending up in the same place. In other words, I hadn't learned anything.

Then it hit me. Or rather, I hit it. That moment when I knew that my best judgment had gotten me to this place and it was a place I absolutely did not want to be. All my decisions had brought me to a time in my life when things should have been much different. And I had no one to blame but myself. So what was I going to do now? Where was my strength? Why did this all happen and how could I get out of here?

I didn't want to play anymore. I was willing to admit that I didn't really understand the rules. I was tired and I wanted someone else to take over. I was finally humble enough to let something greater than me take control of my life. And with that decision came a wave of peace. I had an understanding that was like nothing I had experienced before. There was a blanket of serenity that was placed over my shoulders by the most incredibly warm, loving and tender hands I had ever felt. I breathed a deep breath and knew that this was the best decision I had ever made. And, it was the last decision I ever had to make on my own. Now I had a partner and my partner will always keep me safe from those dead-ends and rock bottoms, as long as I let him do the driving.

****

I am awake!
How long have I been sleeping?
Amazing…
There is so much to do
So much to see
Life is just beginning.
What a wonderful place to be
Here
Now
Awake
Alive
Healthy
Wonderful
Me
There are no limits
There is no time
Action is taking place
So much to experience
And I am doing it
Here
Now
Awake
Alive
Healthy
Wonderful
Me

****

More and more doors open
To the endless possibilities we cannot even know

To the feelings our five sense don't understand
To the places we don't know exist
The journey is just beginning
The death of the old self brings birth to a new life
Let me live my true life
Let me see with new eyes
Let me feel in ways I've never felt
And hear things unheard
Let me taste the unbelievable sweetness of life.

****

Acknowledge the adventure
Acknowledge the journey
Don't miss a moment
Don't miss NOW
See things differently
Have no expectations
Have no judgments
Live life NOW

****

OUR GRANDEUR

We are not afraid that we are inadequate
We are actually afraid that we are tremendously grand
And it becomes hard to hide behind our smallness
Once we have that knowledge

The truth is that we are tremendously grand
We need to know that

We need to live from that place
That is our truth.

Life is grand and we are grand
We can't hide from it forever
Here it is
Right here
Right now
Live it, love it, be it
Start your journey
And be grand!

****

Life is like a video game. You can't advance to the next level unless you master the one you are on.

****

YOUR MUSTARD SEED MOMENT

Are you where you want to be on your journey right now? Do you find that you are disappointed by some of your choices? Are you going down the same path you have gone down before? Or, perhaps you are where you want to be, but you wouldn't mind having a little help with the tough decisions. Either way, maybe it's time for a change. Stop for a few minutes and ask yourself if it is possible that there is a way of looking at things that you have been unwilling or unable to find? Then simply admit this to yourself. Say it out loud, write it down, whisper it, or shout it:
I am willing to see things differently.
I am willing to make different choices.

I am willing to let my light shine brightly.
I am willing to live life the way it was meant to be lived.

Do this every day. After a few days you will feel a difference. Try it. You've got nothing to lose.

Chapter 2

Have A Little Faith

Behind every blade of grass is its very own angel that forever whispers:
"grow...grow."
From the Ethic of Judaism

****

Some of you may have cringed at the title of this chapter. But just think, we practice faith every single day of our lives. Do we go through our day worrying that we could just lift off the ground and float through the air? Or do we have faith that gravity will keep us firmly planted on the ground? Do we go to sleep at night and express concern over whether the sun will come up tomorrow? Or do we have faith that our planet will continue rotating at just the right speed for the sun to rise in the morning? Do we consciously will our blood to travel through our veins and arteries? Or do we have faith that our heart will pump it for us? The examples are endless.

We practice faith every second of every day. Can we remember ever hearing our friends say that they wouldn't take a single step unless someone explained gravity to them? We don't need to know any formulas or concepts to know it works. Yet, often the existence of God has been challenged. We don't need to see radio waves to know that when we turn on the radio we will hear music. But, people ask why they can't see God. The answer is this. To know God, feel God, see God and experience God we first have to have faith.

For me faith is not a conscious effort. It is a knowing; knowing there is a power that is greater than I am. I know that if I let things follow their natural course, they always have a way of working out. I know that when I concentrate on positive thoughts, positive things begin to happen. And I know that the opposite is also true. All of these things go beyond believing. They are a knowing. And while it is hard to explain a knowing, there is no doubt once you've experienced it–literally. A knowing goes beyond all doubt. It is the ultimate level of faith.

We've all heard the expression "leap of faith." Well, in order to experience the vast abundance and endless happiness that are our inherent rights, we must first take that step forward. We must take that leap of faith. Know what waits for us. Know that infinite peace and unconditional love are ours if we just have faith. And watch our fears melt away before our eyes. Where there is faith no fear can exist.

****

THE BLADE OF GRASS

It was January 1st and time for my annual walk on Jones Beach. This walk had traditionally been a time to reflect on the past year as well as dream-build for the future. I looked forward to these walks. The cold ocean air, and the bright sunshine had a way of washing the mind and soul. They brought clarity to my thoughts in a way that nothing else did.

This year was different though. It was the first time in many years that I was making this trip alone. It's one of those old stories of boy meets girl, they think it is forever and somehow it goes wrong. Thoughts of this failed relationship took up most of the reflection portion of my walk. Even though my life took some very positive turns since then, the part of the year that stood out most in my mind was the deep sense of loss, hurt and pain I felt. But I needed to do this. I was letting the icy ocean wind work its magic by chasing each and every one of those heavy thoughts out of my mind and into thin air. It felt great.

The dream building did not come easily this year. So many dreams had fallen apart with the relationship and I couldn't seem to bring myself to start a new one. I still had some doubts. Was I really ready to experience life on all levels again? Did I deserve all the things I wanted? Would I ever find someone who would love me unconditionally? The questions kept coming and the answer I kept sensing was "have faith." For the most part my faith had been unshakeable, but at this moment I was feeling out of sorts and wondering if everything would turn out okay.

Now, everyone who knows me has heard my guardian angel stories. I am convinced that I have at least one, if not a whole flock of guardian angels following me. One of the ways they let me know they are there is to bring a feather to me whenever I am feeling a little low. Sometimes these feathers appear in the most unusual places as if the angels want to prove to me that they are always by my side. This day was no exception.

About the time that I began to question myself, I saw a feather half-buried in the sand. It looked tattered and much worse for wear, but it was a feather. I immediately felt better. I knew that my angels were nearby, making sure I didn't get too low. And then, I noticed another feather, and another, and another. There were dozens of them. Considering how hard the wind was blowing, it was a miracle that these feathers had found a way to anchor themselves so they would not be blown away.

One of the feathers in particular caught my attention. On this part of the beach was some straw-like grass, just managing to hold on against the wind and blowing sand. This feather had flown in such away that the sharp end, the quill, had literally pierced a blade of grass. These two unlikely companions had become one. The feather had united with the grass and together the two were holding on for dear life as the wind whipped them mercilessly. They probably would have stayed like that indefinitely, but curiosity got the better of me. I had to look at it more closely, examine it, study it, and see what was holding these two together. I knew there had to be a lesson in this.

I carefully plucked the grass out of the sand and placed it deep in my pocket. The wind was fierce and I did not want it to blow away. I walked a little more quickly now, anxious to examine my treasure. Once or twice I peeked into my pocket to make sure it was still there. I was returning to my car. It was the best refuge from the wind and icy cold. Somehow the numbness in my toes and fingers wasn't bothering me anymore.

I was only a few yards from my car when it hit me. A strange gust of wind seemed to come from a different direction. It almost made me lose a step. But, that was not what caught my attention. This gust had somehow managed to reach into my pocket and blown my feather away. The feather actually swirled boldly right in front of my face before it blew away. It was like a bad scene from a worse movie. I couldn't believe it. I had wanted so much to look at my prize up close and hopefully come to realize the message in its existence. How was I supposed to do that now that it was gone? And then I understood that I had gotten my message.

This was not a lesson to be learned by sitting and studying a blade of grass with a feather attached to it. I wasn't supposed to analyze it to death, hold it in my hand and study it. There were no answers for me in this type of clinical examination. I was, however, intended to know that somehow, someway, these two objects had come together under great odds. They were united against the elements, against the hardship, against anything that life would send their way. This was the same way that my angels stuck to me. Regardless of the "mess" I had gotten myself into, the angels were always there for me. And they send me feathers to remind me. I was so thankful and my faith was strengthened knowing that they were with me against all odds.

****

We have nothing to lose and everything to gain by having faith in something that is greater than we are. It doesn't matter what we call it and it doesn't matter what our religion is. What does matter is that we stop trying to control everything around us and have faith that all things in the universe are exactly where they should be at this moment. Once we begin to have this faith we will begin to see the glorious dance of life right in front of our eyes. Nothing will seem as it did before and our life will take on a new meaning. In time we will know what our purpose is on this earth. And it all begins by letting go.

****

Follow not the teachings
Know the wisdom
Follow not the footsteps
Know the path

****

Dear God,
I have these moments.
I don't know how to describe them.
But, they don't feel good.
They are moments when I feel wrong
About my life and myself.
I feel small, lonely, tired and
Insignificant.
It doesn't always make sense and
Sometimes it hits me for no reason.
But, God, at those moments I feel so low.
I guess it doesn't matter why it happens.
It does help to know that you are there.
When I am feeling down
And I don't like myself
I am comforted to know you are there.

I know you are gently holding me and telling me
Everything will be okay
Even when I am being less than my best
Thank you for always loving me.
Amen

****

Everything will be okay
And most of all
I know that you will always love me

****

THE MUSTARD SEED WAY

I tried it my way
I had control
I made the decisions
I took the credit
I was proud
Doing it my way
But things didn't seem right
I didn't seem whole.

So, maybe a man would help
That's when I did it his way
He had control
He made the decisions
He took the credit
He was proud
Doing it his way

But things still didn't seem right
We didn't feel whole

And then I tried it the mustard seed way
I gave up control
I asked for guidance in my decisions
I didn't take the credit
I was no longer proud
I was humble
And things began to feel right
Now I felt whole
Because I had the faith to go
The mustard seed way

****

YOUR MUSTARD SEED MOMENT

Start practicing faith in your life. Write down some things that are weighing heavily on your mind and your heart. One by one let them go. You may even want to write them each on separate pieces of paper. As you decide to let your faith take over on each issue, either crumple it up and throw it out, or burn it in a fireplace. Let this symbolism help you to give it away and take it out of your life. Feel how much lighter the world seems as you have the faith to get these issues out of your mind. Keep a journal and write down how this feels. This process may take any amount of time that you feel comfortable with. There is no hurry. It took us years to get to this place and it will take time to get out of it. Have patience with yourself and be good to yourself. You do deserve it.

Chapter 3

Something Greater

"The Word is the lock and the Word is the key. An awakened Word, received from an awaken master, is the only way to awaken the dormant Word in the heart of the sleeping disciple. Upon introducing the Word, the gross inarticulate Word merges into the eternal Word." Guru Goraknatha (Gorakabani 21)

****

There is a place between my cells
That vibrates with the energy of life
With the knowing of what is
And is not
It vibrates through me and around me
Leaving no place untouched
And what seemed solid
Now seems an illusion
Knowing that the same energy
That vibrates through me
Vibrates between the cells of all we know
Hear the pause
See the space

And know something is there
And nothing is there

****

Once when I was a little girl, I got up in the middle of the night to go to the bathroom. I was tired, it was dark and I felt my way down the hall. I just slid my hand along the wall knowing approximately where each door jam was and approximately how far it was to the bathroom.

On the return trip down the hall, I felt a little more confident and didn't use the wall as my guide. About three quarters of the way back to my room I felt a strange sensation to my right–almost like a breeze. I turned in that direction and took several steps forward. Since the hallway is only a few feet wide I knew that I was now standing somewhere else. But, I also knew that there was no doorway in that part of the hall. I didn't feel like I was in a room. It felt much more vast, as if I was standing in a huge cave or even outside under a dark night sky. I felt the sensation more distinctly at that point, as if a soft breeze was touching my face. I definitely was not in a room in the house. But there was darkness and I could not see anything.

There was gentleness in this place, but also an incomprehensible largeness about it. I don't know how long I stood there. It may have been a few seconds or even a few minutes. Time didn't seem to exist. Only peace. After a while I decided to go back to my room. I turned around, took a few steps forward and was in the hallway again. I was only a few feet from my room and in a couple of seconds I was back in bed.

There was a part of me that felt like I should be scared. But I wasn't. I knew I had experienced something extraordinary, something great. I felt special and I felt loved.

****

So, what is this power, this energy, this being? Throughout history there have been so many names for it–God, Allah, Jehovah, Yahweh… Some think of it as the universal consciousness. Some call it the great I am, the Beloved, the Divine, the Creator. Some see it as a female entity and some see it as male. No matter what name you give it or where you experience it, it is the same thing.

Personally, the biggest challenge I had in understanding the concept of God was trying to think of Him as a wise old man sitting in a big chair up in heaven. This was an acceptable image until I was about six years old. And then there was about a twenty-five year gap in which I didn't know what to believe. The wise old man theory wasn't holding up and the other approach of "God is everything" was not working for me either. I knew there was something but I didn't know what.

I could say that I began a quest to find God, but that sounds much more romantic than what actually happened. In reality I ran out of options. Life was not working out no matter how hard I tried and I needed some answers. I needed a direction and most of all I wanted to feel loved. It took a near-death experience and the end of a long relationship to make me cry out to the "God-I-wasn't-sure-of-but-sincerely-hoped-existed."

In that moment, with that decision, came an overwhelming peace. The pain subsided and the sobbing eased and I felt a place in my heart open and fill with a light. I knew I was not alone and had never been alone. I felt good for the first time in years.

No matter how often I try to explain this experience I realize that my words fall too short. How do you express a feeling that goes beyond anything you can imagine? What words do you choose to describe the unlimited and unbounded? We restrict ourselves to five senses but this experience encompasses those five and probably ten more that we don't understand yet.

****

There will never be enough ink

And many trees will be felled
To create the sheets on which
Communication could only touch
The mere tip of fullness that fills
Hearts, heads, souls, lives, worlds
With wonder and joy
A sheer glance is more telling
Than the awkward scribings I use
To tell the oldest tale known to man
And to all creation
But the beauty is no less real
In this knowledge

****

Does this bring you closer to an understanding of God? Maybe, just maybe it will help you to look in places you didn't think of before. Instead of looking to the sky for a godly domain, know that heaven exists here on earth. Maybe instead of thinking of an old man in a big chair think of a small child sitting near you laughing and chatting away. Perhaps you won't look for the answers in words but in the silences between words.

Your mere desire to find God will bring you infinitely closer to the knowing. There is a saying that if you take one step towards God he takes one hundred steps towards you. You can't even imagine what will happen if you take hold of his hand. No eye has seen, no ear has heard, no mind has conceived what God has prepared for those who love him.

****

This music is going through my head. It is magnificent. It is like the sound right before a concert when all the instruments are warming up. The clarinet is playing a scale. The stringed instruments are all blending together except for the one cello that is playing arpeggios. And there are percussive sounds randomly punctuating the musical sentences. I am just waiting for the TAP, TAP, TAP, TAP of the conductor's baton on his music stand.

There it is…

TAP, TAP, TAP

And all falls quiet. Then comes the inherent anticipation. What is the program? Will I like it? Am I in the right concert hall? Did I get the right address? When will it start? I am poised between the baton tap and the music. And suddenly there are no more doubts. I am no longer uncomfortable. I settle into my seat. I become filled with joyous anticipation and a peace. I know the music will be beautiful because I recognize the conductor.

****

YOUR MUSTARD SEED MOMENT

Take a walk through the woods and appreciate the beauty that surrounds you. Stop often and look closely at the pine needles on the ground or the bark of the tree. Really let yourself experience the fullness that exists in nature. If you already believe in God, this will allow you to appreciate his presence in your life. If you are just contemplating the existence of something greater, a nature walk is a terrific time to understand the grandness of what surrounds us. Remember, this is not a marathon. Take many breaks, breathe deeply and smile often.

Chapter 4

Finding Peace

Om Mani Padme Hum

"The jewel of consciousness is in the heart's lotus"

When heart and mind are united, anything is possible.

****

How do we learn to quiet the mind
And listen to the song of the soul?
How do we learn to let go of the past
And let love be our only goal?

Now is the time to change our ways
To let love lead our heart and our mind.
Stop being afraid of what we can't see
And know God is infinitely kind.

The world is in need of spirits like ours
And we know we must play out our role.
So, now we will learn to quiet the mind
And hear the song of the soul.

****

Sometimes my head is filled with so many ideas and I realize that I need to quiet it down. There is a whirl of thoughts and feelings and I try to find that place in the center of it all. I don't try to control it. I just consciously bring myself to that place. The choice I make is not to be a part of the chaos. It is a choice I make to view the world from a place of peace. This is the place where we can know the truth and hear the song of the soul. In this silence I feel closest to God.

We knew this as children. We watched events unfold before us and in no way tried to participate in the unfoldment or judgment. We merely watched, took unbiased notes and went on with our lives. Unfortunately, somewhere along the way our egos kick in and insist that we join in the "mess." We become aware that we have the power to change events and this power becomes addictive. Before we know it we are far from the beautiful place of peace we knew, with no map to return.

The good news is that we can revisit that place and if we want we can live there permanently. But there are choices to make. There is work to be done. We can't undo years of decisions overnight. This undoing or unlearning takes time. Just know that it can be done and with practice we can find peace.

One method I use on a daily basis to help achieve that silence, that peace, is meditation. There are many different types of meditation and you need to find the one that is most comfortable for you. But regardless of which one you choose, the ultimate goal is to stop the chatter in your brain. We all need to halt that incessant cycle of thought that run over and over in your mind. We want to experience a calm, a peace. And in that state we can connect with the universe and connect with God.

Before I meditate, I prepare myself mentally and physically. I unplug the phone, turn off the television and radio. I put on comfortable clothes and sometimes I light incense and candles. None of these steps are necessary; however, I find that it helps me get into the right frame of mind. I am mindful of each part of this preparation. I know that I am getting myself ready to spend a few minutes of precious quiet time. This time is invaluable and I treat it as such.

Depending on what type of meditation you choose, you may sit up, lie down, chant, stay silent, follow guided imagery, open your eyes or close them. There is no right or wrong. Regardless of the details, two elements should be consistent. The first is breathing and the second is eliminating the chatter.

Breathing is a vital part of life and meditation. Besides the obvious need to take oxygen into our bodies, we also eliminate waste products when we exhale. Much of our day is spent in shallow breathing, and now is a good time to concentrate on taking in entire lung-fulls of life sustaining oxygen. Then exhale all the toxins from deep in your lungs. Long slow breathes feel so relaxing and healthy. And the other benefit is that when we put our concentration on our breathing, we are able to start the process of quieting our thoughts.

Why do we need to silence our minds? What is the purpose of clearing our brains of chatter? It reminds me of the scene from <u>Little Red Riding Hood</u> when she says to the wolf, disguised as her Grandmother, "Grandma, what big ears you have." To this the wolf answers, "The better to hear you with." Eliminating the noise allows us to hear better.

Have you ever been at a concert where the music and crowd were so loud that you could not hear the person standing next to you? That is essentially what is happening to you right now. You are so close to being able to "hear" the song of the soul. You just need to decide to turn your brain off for a while. Don't try to fight with your thoughts. Don't get angry with yourself if it is difficult to stop thinking. Just gently push the thoughts to the side and look for that space between the thoughts. Concentrate on non-thought.

This process takes time and discipline. It can be very frustrating in the beginning. If you are uncomfortable after a few minutes of meditation, just stop. Next time try to sit quietly for a few minutes more. As time goes on you will become more comfortable and the stillness will come easier.

(There are also times when it is not easy, but you know how great the benefits are and you will want to wait it out.) Soon you will be meditating 20 minutes, 40 minutes, even an hour. You will find that as you get better, time will seem to go much faster. You will feel like you've only been there 10 minutes and when you look at the clock it will be much longer. This sense of timelessness can become a common experience.

Meditation is good for so many reasons. It helps you find a peaceful place within yourself, and it brings you to a state where you are more receptive to hearing the messages of the universe. When you practice meditation with consistency and discipline you will find that you need less sleep. And, studies are being done about the many other medical benefits of meditation.

****

Unspoken silence so very tangible
I can practically touch and feel its presence
The fullness of that moment that still goes
Unspoken but real
Comforted by the knowing
Yet anxious in the thought
That the unspoken silence may be broken
Shattering what is perfect in sheer knowledge
But becomes mundane through words
Uttered so all who hear them will know
What is already known
Truth need not be limited by our need
To confine it in words
Communication is our claim in these efforts
But what we are losing is the deep sense
That tells us, yes
Through the silence a resounding yes is felt

Or heard or both together
In a way that is undeniable and
Inexpressible with the words we use
As lassos of meanings and feelings
When our heart could flourish in the
Unspoken silence, Unspoken silence
That fills the void that once was
In my heart but no longer exists because
It is now filled with the unconditional and unspoken.

****

Om—the sound of the universe
It is in the wind
It is in the rustling leaves
And in the running stream
The world speaks and it says Om
It is in everything and everything in it.

Imagine a moment where everything stopped
For just a moment
And in that moment
Everything said Om
In that moment all would last forever
It would be a moment in which we would know our unity
We would know our oneness.
We are one with each other.
We are one with the universe.
Om.
Shalom.

****

Dear Creator,
It is my desire to be a living example
Of peace and tranquility.
In this world it seems so difficult
To find these qualities.
Please help me to live it.
I want others to know
Peace is possible
Peace is real
Peace exists.
My life has been far from peaceful.
But through the pain
I have always founds peace.
Please let me bring peace to others.
Amen

****

Dear Beloved,
The only way I can bring peace to the world
Is if I find peace within myself.
Please help me to find that place
The place inside that no thing can touch
And no one can hurt.
I know it is there.
I remember.
Let me live from that place.
Let me live in that peace.
Amen

****

YOUR MUSTARD SEED MOMENT

Take an opportunity to treat your mind to the wonderful sound of silence. Set aside 20 minutes with no television, radio or phone. Light some candles and turn the lights down. If you have hesitation, remember that it is not the silence you fear. It is what you say to yourself in that silence that frightens you. So, be still. Quiet your mind. Learn to make peace with yourself and with others. It can change your life

Chapter 5

Don't Forget To Say Your Prayers

It is impossible for us to always know what is best. We can only see our tiny part of the picture. Prayer allows us to ask for what is best, even if it is not what we expect.

****

For some people meditation will seem unnatural or uncomfortable. In this case, don't practice it. But, if you are still looking for a way to find more peace in your life, then you will want to think about praying. If you are able to incorporate both meditation and prayer into your life then you have a powerful combination. I like to think of prayer as a way of throwing some questions and thoughts out into the universe. Meditation allows me to be quiet enough to hear the reply.

Praying is a regular part of my life; and now that I am more comfortable with it, I have moments of prayer throughout my day. Don't worry, I don't throw myself down on my knees, clutch my hands together and stare towards heaven in the middle of the mall. But I do designate a few specific times each day for my God chat. In addition I manage to sprinkle some impromptu prayers when the mood strikes me. Actually, I've gotten to the point where I have an ongoing conversation with God. It has brought me great peace.

What time of the day is good for prayer? Any time is wonderful, but the two times I designate specifically is when I wake up and right before I go to sleep. I try not to start my day unless I have 15-30 minutes of reflection/meditation/prayer. On days when I skip these, there is a noticeable difference.

I know, I know, I hear it already. "Who has time in the morning to pray?" Well, I believe you can't afford not to make time, even if it's in the shower, or driving the car or scrambling eggs. How about in between the time the alarm goes off and the next time you hit the snooze button? Those few moments can change the entire complexion of the day.

Very often my morning prayer consists of projections for the day and its events. As I go over these plans silently (or out loud if you want) I run it all by God and ask for guidance as each situation arises. And boy, is he agreeable. He has never said "no" to me yet. I ask him to help me as I go through my day and then have faith that he will be there. My day starts so much better when I take the burden off myself and know that I can trust my partner.

The moments right before I go to sleep is especially magical. Sometimes I pray the "old-fashioned" method. I get down on my knees next to my bed, fold my hands and pray. But, I can't tell you how many times I woke up with comforter creases on my face after falling asleep in that position. Mostly I just climb into bed, fluff up my pillows, fold my hands and talk to God. I just talk to him. At least now I do.

It wasn't always that easy for me. When I first started praying I needed something more structured. The kind that begins with "Dear God" and ends with "Amen." I remembered a prayer I learned when I was a child and said that for a while until I got more creative. The prayer went like this:

God made the sun
God made the tree
God made the mountain
And God made me.
I thank you, oh God
For the sun and the tree
For making the mountain

And for making me.
Amen

It worked. It got me thinking about being grateful and taking my eyes off myself. And best of all, it got me talking to God.

After a few days I was able to start making up my own prayers. If this doesn't come easily for you, don't worry. We've often been told that talking to ourselves means we are crazy, and until we get used to it, praying can feel like we are talking to ourselves. But believe me, you are not. Prayer is an incredibly powerful form of communication. You are communicating with the Devine, the power that can form the universe, the energy that moves us and shapes us, the everything that is and is not. After some of the mundane chatter we have during the day, this is truly a special time.

What happens if you fall asleep while you are praying? Don't worry. I think this makes it even more special. I believe that the thoughts you carry with you from consciousness to sleep spread wings and fly with wild abandon into the universe. For this reason you may want to be careful what you pray about.

Praying is a good time to be thankful for our many blessings. It is a time to be grateful for the things we have and those we don't have. It is a time to reflect on the ways we can be helpful and caring. It is a time to ask how we can serve the world. And it is a time to build our friendship with God. I have come to rely on that friendship completely and implicitly and I know my prayers are what make that relationship possible.

Some of you may be old pros at praying and some of you may not. If you need a few suggestions to get you going, I've included a few different types of prayers. If they feel good for you, use them. If not, they can serve as guidance. Once you master these, it will become easier to continue your conversations with God throughout the day. It will also make it possible for you to be more aware of life around you. You will begin to look for the answers to your prayers in the events happening during your day. You will see how people, places and things all come together in the dance of life, to bring God's messages. There are no coincidences. Everything happens for a reason. So pray away and wait for the universe to create the answers to those prayers. Have fun watching life unfold around you.

****

Dear Beloved,
There is so much on my mind this morning.
I am trying to find a calm place in the center of it all.
Please help me to find it.
Please help me to know your peace.
Please help me to face the day with a calm spirit.
With you by my side I know that all things are possible.
Amen

****

Dear I am,
Here it is, Sunday night.
A new week is almost here.
I have so many plans and so much to do.
So, before I begin it
I want to ask for your help.
Please guide me through each day.
Let me see things through your eyes.
If challenges come up, please let me face them calmly.
Don't let me get too serious.
I want to know the light side of life too.
Let the people I come across feel better for our meeting.
Let me leave the earth a little better each day.
Thank you, dear Lord, for your constant guidance and support.
I love you.

Amen

****

Dear Heavenly Father,
I thank you for another day.
As I prepare myself for sleep
I review the day and think about tomorrow.
Please use me tomorrow as you did today.
Maybe I can make one person laugh
Or one person smile.
Maybe I'll wipe a tear
Or give a hug.
Or, maybe I'll just be there to listen.
Whatever your will is, dear Lord.
I trust in your guidance and love.
Amen

****

Dear Heavenly Mother,
I begin this day with thoughts of you.
Please guide me through the day
With your gentle hand.
Lead me on the paths that will best serve your purpose.
Allow me to treat each person I meet with love.
May these people then bring the love they have received
And pass it on to anyone in their path.
Thank you, dear God, for filling me with your peace and grace.
I live in your love.
Amen
****

Dear Lord,
I pray for peace tonight.
As I prepare for sleep
I know that I will wake tomorrow
Well rested and ready for a new day.
But many will not.
So many people are battling in so many ways.
I pray, dear God, that tonight
For just a moment
Everyone that is uneasy
Will feel your peace.
May your light and love
Find a place to enter into their darkness –
Even if only for a second.
Tomorrow will be a much better day
When everyone knows your love.
Amen

****

Dear Jehovah,
Today is New Year's Day.
I woke up this morning feeling like I had a new beginning.
A fresh start.
What a wonderful gift.
I can stop bad habits
And begin new ones.
I can be happy and healthy.
I can start new projects and finish the ones I've put off.
I can do so many things I've been meaning to do.
And, dear God, one of those things
I've been meaning to do

Is start each day as if
It's New Year's Day.
Every day offers a new beginning and a fresh start.
I pray that I remember this every morning when I wake up.
I pray that I treat each day as the gift it is.
Amen

****

Dear Allah,
I give my life to you.
In this way I know that
My thoughts, words and actions
Will be guided by you.
When I have to make a decision
I will stop, ask for your advice
And then listen.
You have always answered my prayers.
I know you always will.
I just need to let go of the thought
That I have control.
I trust in your strength
And I know you will always guide me
In the right direction.
Thank you, dear God.
Amen

****

YOUR MUSTARD SEED MOMENT

Wherever you are right now, stop and say a prayer. It can be funny, it can be sad, it doesn't matter. Just start a conversation with God. It may seem one-sided right now, but that's okay. Just take time to talk to your higher power. Once you get started you will probably find that you have a lot to say. Go ahead, unload. It feels good.

Chapter 6

A Sense Of Gratitude

Throughout my day and especially during prayer, I express my gratitude. I find it tremendously fulfilling to spend time listing the things in my life for which I am grateful. Somehow the challenges seem smaller when I stack up all the wonders. Also, I want God to know how thankful I am. I want the message to go out loud and clear that I don't take any of my blessings for granted. This practice has made me more aware of the abundance in my life and has made me much happier.

Stop for a moment and look at your surroundings. List ten things right now that you are grateful for. In case you have a difficult time with this, here is my list:

- I am thankful for this chair I am sitting on because I don't want to sit on the floor.
- I am thankful for my pen and paper so I can express my feelings through the written word.
- I am thankful for the table in front of me holding the items I need.
- I am thankful for the bottle of water I am drinking so I won't be thirsty.
- I am thankful for the lights so I can see clearly.
- I am thankful for the shoes that keep my feet warm and protected.
- I am thankful for the air conditioning that is keeping the temperature comfortable.
- I am thankful for my hand holding the pen as I write.

- I am thankful for my eyes allowing me to see all the wonders around me.
- I am thankful for the air I am breathing.

How did you do? Was it hard? I found that I took many things for granted and I didn't want to do that anymore. I wanted to be more aware of everything around me. That's why I started doing this exercise regularly. Try doing it daily. If you want to, write them down, and add a few every time. When life gets you down, just pull out your list and reflect on your blessings.

I am reminded of the scene from "The Sound of Music." Maria is in her bedroom when a thunderstorm starts. One by one the children appear at her door from the youngest to the oldest. They all are frightened by the thunder and lightening. Instead of telling them that there is nothing to be frightened of, Maria tells them what she does when something upsets her. In those times of stress she lists her favorite things. You may have heard her list before.

Raindrops on roses
Whiskers on kittens
Bright copper kettles
Warm woolen mittens
Brown paper packages
Tied up with string
These are few of my favorite things.

How can you help but smile and feel better when you think of that list?

Notice that the storm didn't suddenly stop and Maria didn't tell the children that they are foolish for being frightened. All she did was take their attention away from something upsetting and put it on something pleasant. We can choose to do that too. But, that is the key. You need to make the choice to move your attention for what is upsetting and think about things that make you happy.

Once again, this may not be an easy practice for most people. We are so bombarded by bad news on a regular basis that it is hard to believe that there is much to be thankful for. Many conversations revolve around what is wrong with this world instead of what's right. I have actually excused myself from some of those conversations because it is my choice not to be around a lot of negativity. I am what Robert Schuller calls a "possibility thinker." I like to see the possibilities in every situation.

Try spending one day just being aware of your thoughts and the conversations around you. If something violent is on the television, turn to another channel. If there is something on the radio that is upsetting, change stations. Only read the pages of newspapers and magazines that are light-hearted and positive. If something negative is coming up in a conversation, try to turn it around to see the other side. Choose positive input for your brain. There is so much in this world to be grateful for that it is a shame to miss it for all the negativity. So, give it a shot. Make someone smile today, starting with youself. Have fun and be grateful.

****

I saw violets growing between the cracks in the sidewalk.
It made me smile.
Those beautiful little flowers
Purple and yellow and white
Flourishing in the most unlikely place
How often have I felt like those violets?
How often have I felt I was striving to beat all odds?
How often have I felt I was surrounded
By coldness–hard and ungiving?
But somehow, somehow
When I felt as if I would just wither and die
And it seemed like there was nowhere to grab hold
I did
I did
I grabbed hold the soil of my faith

And the water of love
And I bloomed
Against the odds, I bloomed
I thank God for all the flowers
But especially the beautiful little violets
Growing in the concrete.

****

I am sitting in the backyard getting a little sun and fresh air. If I stretched my left big toe out a little bit I can touch the small white eggplant that is hanging in the vegetable garden. The cicadas are very loud and occasionally I see one of their large bodies fly by and land clumsily on a plant. The weight of the insect bends the leaf at an uncomfortable angle and you wait for it to snap off or the cicada to fall. There is nothing attractive about these bugs. I thought they only came around every seven years. Did someone forget to tell them?

As I look at the vegetable garden (which is really more of a patch than a garden), I see an earthworm moving over an area of soil where the sun has found a way between the leaves. How unusual to see an earthworm above the ground, alive. The only time I usually see them is drowned in a puddle after a rainstorm. It is catching my eye because the sun is glistening on its moist body. It is gliding by, moving clumps of dirt that are in its way. I never thought I would see the beauty in a worm. But there it is, going about its business and moving for that brief moment through a place in my world. It is gone now, oblivious to the fact that it had an admirer.

The ugly cicadas and the glistening earthworm have both brightened my day. It is in the small, unexpected events that I experience great joy. No expectations, no plan, just witnessing and knowing.

****

I am overcome by your presence. I am overcome by your love. It leaves me speechless. It leaves me with tears. All I have ever needed is here. All I have ever searched for is now. There is no longer a hole in my heart because it is filled with your love. I feel no more loneliness because you are by my side. I know no more fear because you are here.

Thank you for the knowing. Thank you for the remembering. Thank you for guiding me home. Thank you, dear God. Thank you for the love.

I will wear your cloak of love out into the world. I will bring your message of peace to those who will listen. I will bring the beauty of your presence to those who will see. I will touch the hearts of those who will feel. Let me wear the cloak well.

Thank you, dear God, for your words and your wisdom. Thank you for your strength and your love.

****

I end another day with a smile on my face. It is the most warm and wonderful feeling to know I am loved and cared for. I am thankful that I finally understand this. So many years went by without this understanding, this appreciation, this knowing. But now it is different. I will never take another thing for granted. I will live from this place of love.

****

Life is good right now.
So much seems to be going in the right direction.
I am excited about the many prospects that are ahead of me.
I feel like I have endless possibilities and the sky is the limit.
And not even the sky is the limit.
I am thankful for all that I have
And for all that I don't have.
What a wonderful time to be alive.
What a wonderful time to feel alive.

****

Dear God,
Thank you for this day
Thank you for my friends
Thank you for my job
Thank you for my sense of humor
Thank you for your guidance.
Thank you for my car
Thank you for my home
Thank you for my health
Thank you for your blessings
Thank you for my dream
Thank you for my ambition
Thank you for my talents
Thank you for my feet
Thank you for my hands
Thank you for my eyes
Thank you for my mouth
Thank you for my ears
Thank you for my body
Thank you for my family
Thank you for my life
Thank you for my shoes
Thank you for strength
Thank you for wisdom
Thank you for humility
Thank you for love
Thank you for everything
Amen

****

YOUR MUSTARD SEED MOMENT

If you haven't written your list of the ten things you are grateful for, do it now. Put the list in a place where you can add to it on a regular basis. After a while you will find that you have a tremendous amount in your life to be grateful for. Even the things that seemed like a burden at one point may eventually end up on your gratitude list. You may be surprised!

Chapter 7

Be Childlike

I don't believe that the more years your body has been on this earth the more boring and stuffy you have to be. If that's what acting your age means, then I never intend to do it. No way. Now don't misunderstand me. I don't condone being immature, childish or petty. I do, however, strongly recommend seeing the world every day, every moment, as if you are looking through the eyes of a child. The world suddenly transforms to a magnificent and magical place.

One of my favorite passages from the Bible is Mark 10:13-16:

"People were bringing little children to Jesus to have him touch them, but the disciples rebuked them. When Jesus saw this he was indignant. He said to them, 'Let the little children come to me and do not hinder them, for the Kingdom of God belongs to such as these. I tell you the truth, anyone who will not receive the Kingdom of God like a little child will never enter it' And he took the children in his arms, put his hands on them and blessed them."

Well, I have every intention of being in heaven, so I am packing my crayons and going. What about you?

You may ask what it means to "receive the Kingdom of God like a child." The first newsflash is that you already are in the Kingdom of God. Here it is. Look around right now. Surprised? Many people are because they think they have lots of time to prepare before they die and go to heaven. But the revelation is that it is here. No need to die. And no need to wait to experience it. It is time to be "like a little child" now.

Being childlike means that you don't see in limits. It is okay to color outside of the lines. Being childlike means that you see the good in others before the bad. It is okay to say hello to strangers. Being childlike means you live from love, not fear. It is okay to open your heart unconditionally. Being childlike means that you are optimistic. It is okay to expect a gift-wrapped package to be waiting for you on any occasion. Being childlike means that you have good self-esteem. When someone says you are great, it is okay to smile and say, "I know." Being childlike means you believe in oneness. It is okay to use all the crayons in the box in one drawing. Being childlike means you know you don't have all the answers. It is okay to get down on your knees and pray with all your heart and soul. Being childlike means you have a sense of humor. It is okay to tell a joke and then laugh harder than anyone else around you. Being childlike means you have a sense of humility. It is okay to say you are sorry if you hurt someone's feelings. Being childlike means you have endless compassion. It is okay to bring an injured bird into your home and nurse it back to health. Being childlike means you are flexible in body. It is okay to take a nice long brisk walk early in the morning. Being childlike means you are flexible in mind. It is okay to go with the flow when plans have been changed; just expect the best whatever you do. Being childlike means you don't believe you will ever die. It is okay to believe in eternal life. Being childlike means you can experience boundless joy. It is okay to feel happiness that tickles your toes, moves all the way up to the ends of your hair and even makes your teeth tingles. Being childlike means you can practice unconditional forgiveness. It is okay to take that mental tally sheet of everyone who has wronged you and throw it in your imaginary wastebasket. Being childlike means you have tons of confidence. It is okay to walk up to that person you've admired from a distance and tell them how great you think he is. Being childlike means you are seeing things for the first time. It is okay to make a date with your spouse and carry on as if you first met.

So, the next time you are flipping through the channels on your television, watch some cartoons for a while. Or, how about cutting your sandwich on the diagonal and making soup out of your ice cream. There are so many ways to keep life light and fun. Why be so serious all the time? Enjoy the moment and be childlike.

****

A light snow was beginning to fall and I decided to bundle up and take a walk around the neighborhood. This was a walk that I took several times a week in nice weather, but in the winter I made this trip far less frequently. So, with hat, scarf, mittens, coat and boots on I ventured out into the snowy evening.

During the past few weeks we had had some snow. There were a few inches on the ground already, but it was mostly found on the lawns. The sidewalks and roads had been cleared, making the walk pretty easy.

There is nothing like a walk at night while snow is falling. It is so peaceful, so gentle. It makes me feel peaceful and gentle with myself, and the world. As I walked, I thought about recent events in my life. The thoughts flowed very comfortably with no sense of irritation or judgment. It was a stream of consciousness and I was enjoying the thoughts and the walk. As a matter of fact, I was so deep in thought that I was half way through my walk before I realized that the snow had turned to rain.

It was a light rain, rather like a mist, and my coat was already pretty wet. It must have been raining for a while because the snow on the ground was turning slushy at this point. It was then that I noticed some footprints on the ground. They were facing in the other direction and they were small–like those of a child. As I walked I kept looking at the small footprints that were going the other way. I wondered what a child could be doing out on a night like this walking alone around the neighborhood. It was probably past his or her bedtime and it was rather cold to be out. But after a few more steps I realized that the footsteps were my own. Since I was more than half way through my walk I had circled back and was on the same street again. I smiled. I was the child walking in the snow.

At that moment I felt like a child. All the serious thoughts had vanished from my head and I thought of myself as a kid again. I practically started skipping because I felt so light. I felt so free.

As I reached the park I tried to build a snowman. Wouldn't that be cute if people drove by the park in the morning and saw a snowman standing there? But the rain had formed a hard crust on top of the snow and I had to scrap that plan. I was left with just a small snowball in my hand, the embryo of my snowman. I didn't know what to do with it, so I threw it. Then I made another one and ate it. What next? I looked around to see what other wonders were in this winter wonderland. The swings and slide were wet and rather uninviting. And then I thought of making snow angels. That would be fun.

No sooner had the thought entered my head than I fell straight back onto the snowy ground. I must have been a sight with my arms and legs flailing in the snow. But my angel came out so beautifully. I've never seen one like it. I imagined that someone walking their dog in the morning would see it and wonder if a real angel had been there. That's how perfect it was.

By this time I was pretty well soaked. Fortunately I wasn't far from home. Within minutes I was standing in my warm kitchen peeling off the layers of wet clothing knowing that they would leave puddles on the floor. And all the time I was thinking how happy I was, to have seen the footprints in the snow.

****

Dear God,
The eyes of the children reflect
The innocence of the world.
How do we remember that?
The touch of a small hand
Shows the trust we once had.
Can we recapture that?
And the laughter!

Oh, the wonderful laughter of a child
Reminds us of the happiness we knew.
Will we feel that laughter again?
Dear Lord, each day I pray that I see the world
Through the eyes of a child,
That I remember to trust with the instinct of a child,
And that I can laugh,
Truly laugh with the abandon of a child.
That is a great day.
Amen

****

YOUR MUSTARD SEED MOMENT

Spend a day with a child. If you have your own child, it is easy. If you don't, spend time with the child of a friend or relative. During your day, try to see everything as if you are looking through his or her eyes. Take a child to a movie, or an amusement park. Do something you might not usually do. Laugh a lot. Tell silly jokes. Make funny noises. Remember what it was like to be young and then be young.

Chapter 8

I Forgive You

I have never been able to give one of those blood-curdling screams that you hear in the movies. I've been accused of having a high-pitched voice on occasion, but that's the extent of it. Despite the fact that I don't have this talent, I can tell you that for months, during my depression, I heard just such a scream in my head. There were times when it was quieter and farther away, but other times it was so intense that I could actually feel my own throat get soar. I often lost my own voice during this time and my friends would ask why. I told them that it was because I was tired. And that wasn't far from the truth. I was tired of the scream that wouldn't go away.

That scream symbolized much of what I was feeling. It was a scream of pain and anger, guilt and confusion, sadness and loss, resentment and frustration. It started somewhere deep inside and seemed to gather momentum as it rushed through my body. And it was smart. It knew how to grab hold of every painful memory that it could find and bring them all along to remind me just how bad I felt. It was a junk collector and the collection was all too familiar. It was all the garbage I had carelessly left cluttering up my mind and now it was being used as ammunition against me. Oh why hadn't I made peace with all those people and events? Why had I held on to my junk for so long? Why hadn't I learned to forgive them all and toss those terrible memories away?

Aha? Had this scream actually brought me to an awareness? I knew I couldn't live with it much longer. And I knew it grew stronger and louder with the ammunition that I was giving it. I was actually sabotaging myself by keeping so many unloving thoughts around. Well, I was going to show my scream who was boss around here. I was going to throw out all of my junk so it didn't have so much to use against me. I was going to forgive all the people I felt had wronged me, starting with myself. I would make peace with events that should have been long forgotten. And that is where the miracle happened.

As it says in <u>A Course in Miracles</u>, forgiveness is the home of miracles. Now, for those who haven't tried it yet, this isn't an easy concept. I know that it wasn't for me. I felt that if I forgave everyone, then I was being a pushover. I was being a wimp and not standing up for my rights. And, there are plenty of people that I believed didn't deserve my forgiveness. But then I learned that forgiveness was not as much for them as it was for me. Forgiveness does not say that you agree with what others have done. We don't have to condone their actions and we don't have to welcome them back into our lives if we don't want to. However, forgiveness does allow us to see someone else as our brother. It lets us understand that we don't have to stand in judgment of others, and we don't have to crucify them for their actions. It allows us to make peace. It allows our wounds to heal.

Now the work began. It seemed that my scream was loudest in the morning. I would be standing in the shower and wretched thoughts would go through my head. I would think of the people in my life who had annoyed, upset, and hurt me. It was not a great way to start the day. I would walk out of the door each morning with a scowl on my face and a list of people I didn't want to see or speak to. I needed to turn this around. I needed to change my thoughts. So, as I got in the shower I started a new ritual. As the ugly thoughts would come into my head, I would stop, picture the people who were upsetting me and visualize them surrounded by light. I would see them in my mind standing with a beautiful glow bathing their body. And all the while I was bathing my own body. With this picture in my mind I would then sing a song I learned in church. It was a simple little song that I could repeat over and over until I felt better about the person. When I got out of the shower after this new ceremony I felt much cleaner and happier than I had before. Don't misunderstand me. The scream didn't just go away over night. It took months to completely soothe the wounds that I had. And I had a long list of people with whom I had to resolve some issues. But considering that it had taken me years to get to this point, I was willing to wait a few months.

My showers became a time of healing and cleansing in more ways than one. But you may choose to do a similar ritual while you are washing the dishes or driving the car. The important thing is that you find a way to forgive people and let peace enter where hurtful thoughts were before. I can tell you that my scream has gone away and has not come back. It doesn't have any more ammunition. Life is a lot happier now.

****

I am sitting on a bench overlooking the water. I just had lunch at a vegetarian restaurant and I am enjoying life right now. The sparrows are darting back and forth from the grass to the bushes. The sun is shining and the air is warm and fresh. There is a bottle cap on the ground next to the bench. Inside the cap it says in big bold letter: SORRY TRY AGAIN. I laugh because I feel as if I've gotten that bottle cap handed to me a few times in my life. But, isn't that what the journey is all about? I find comfort, knowing that in most cases you can just try again. As we said in our childhood games, we get a "do-over." The challenge is to not waste time lamenting our losses or feeling sorry for ourselves. We need to move on, move on, move on. No sense in watching the parade pass by if you can be a part of it. Let go of past pains and hurt feelings. Just pick yourself up, brush yourself off, and TRY AGAIN.

****

Dear "Person–Who–Hurt–Me,"

There was a moment when I felt more like poking you with this pen than writing you a letter, but the more I thought about it, the more I realized that I needed to get these feelings on paper. So here it is.

When you did the thing you did, it made me feel very badly about myself. I became angry and upset because no one should be treated that way. I wanted to scream and yell and tell you how horrible I thought you were for being so inconsiderate of my feelings. I wanted to find a way to make you feel just as badly. And then I stopped.

These horrible thoughts were consuming me. They were taking up too much of my time, and my anger was getting worse, not better. It was beginning to affect my health. I wanted to find a way to be happy again. Here is what I decided. I decided to forgive you.

Please understand I do not condone your actions. I still think they were hurtful and rude. And I may or may not continue to let you be a part of my life. I will decide that at another time. But I can tell you that I will no longer stand in judgment of you. I will no longer think about ways to hurt you. I will no longer let thoughts of you take up space in my mind. I would rather find peace than live in this hell. For my own sanity and happiness I forgive you. Your actions no longer have any affect on me. I can choose happiness over anger and that is what I choose now.

So, "Person–Who–Hurt–Me," I wish you well and hope you find peace in your heart. I know that I have peace in mine.

Sincerely,

One–Who–Chose–To–Forgive

****

I took inventory and it was painful
I saw my mistakes

I realized how self-destructive I had been
Very sobering
How did I get here?
How do I get out?
When did this all happen?
How could I do this to myself?

Short of a slap in the face
I decided to stop and look forward
Reality check done
Priority check done
Habits are changed
Focus is reestablished
It's time to try this again

Here I go
One step in front of the other
Taking inventory more regularly
But this time it's an inventory of blessings
I'm learning forgiveness
I have new horizons before me
New companions beside me
And new confidence inside me.

****

YOUR MUSTARD SEED MOMENT

Write a letter to someone who has upset you. You don't need to send it, but you do need to let them know how you feel. Express your anger, hurt, sorrow, regret, sadness, and fear. Then forgive them. Write it down. When the letter is done you may decide to save it and read it over to remind yourself that you forgive them. You may decide to burn it to symbolize that you are letting go of your hurt. You may decide to send it. Whatever you decide is okay. The most important part is genuinely learning to forgive someone. After you have written this letter, write one more. In this letter forgive yourself.

Chapter 9

The Greatest Of These Is Love

Love is not something you look for and find. Love is something you are. It is not something that is hiding around the corner waiting to jump out at you. Love is with you always. It doesn't come in the shape of a heart and taste like chocolate. Love is something you breathe. It sustains life in a way that food and water cannot. It opens doors and dimensions that you forgot existed. Love can change everything that you are or think you are. Love cradles every cell in your body and runs through your veins. It is the very essence of who you are now and will be forever. There is nothing that is not love. Love is all.

If you think of love as something that can be quantified, you are not thinking of the true essence of love. True unconditional love cannot be described as bigger, smaller, greater or lesser. You cannot love one thing less and another more. You cannot give one person a little love and another a lot. If you think you can, then you are not describing love. It may be what you have been taught love is, but it is not love. Unconditional love is given to all equally. You can't help it. It is not a choice or an option. It is everyone's inherent right.

Most of us have come to think of love as a romantic feeling that includes hearts, roses and butterflies in the stomach. Very often this is short-lived. Once we realize that our "perfect" person is really human, we lose interest. Some people get beyond this stage of infatuation and begin the work of making a more lasting relationship. With persistence, acceptance, cooperation, compassion, forgiveness, hope, tears, laughter, patience, vision, and a few dozen more qualities, two people can endure many decades together. And for many, this is what love is.

While I am not denying that love does play a part in relationships, relationships themselves do not cause us to feel love. A relationship can bring out feelings that we may not have realized on our own, and it can raise issues that we would not have raised by ourselves. But the relationship itself cannot and does not make us feel loved. Love begins within ourselves and once we have that, the relationship can reflect it back to us. Relationships will always mirror the feelings you have about yourself. So start with loving yourself and the rest will take care of itself.

How do we get to that point? How do we feel love and know love in the truest sense? You begin by knowing that you are loved. At this moment, in this place, you are absolutely and unconditionally loved just as you are. As hard as it is for some to believe, it is the truth. There are some who will not only resist believing this truth, they will actually consider it a blatant lie. For those of you who do not know or acknowledge this love, there is work to be done. Remember, to experience love in any area of your life, truly experience love, you need to know that you are absolutely, positively, unconditionally, 100% loved right now, right here. It is so!

Please know that it doesn't matter who you are or what you have done. Time, place and details are irrelevant in the concept I am talking about. Let go of the idea that you can only be loved if you are a straight A student, or a perfect wife, or have curly red hair, or any of the millions of other variables we can throw out here. None of these things matter at all. You are perfect and loved just as you are.

Your place on this earth is as important as anyone else's. You are a divine being and as such it is your inherent right to be unconditionally loved. You were created in the image of God and this makes you perfect. Period. If you want to argue with this you are only trying to continue your suffering. Perhaps you like to feel small and unworthy, but know this is your choice and your choice alone. Once you accept your perfection and the love that is yours you can begin to experience true love, but not before. You choose.

For those of you who already accept the unconditional love that the universe offers you, you also have work to do. But this is a different kind of work. The work you need to do is give back the love you have received and keep the cycle going. It's an amazing principal. Giving and receiving are actually the same. How can that be, you say? Because everything you send out into the universe comes back to you in abundance. At first you may not recognize the form in which it comes back, but if you have faith in the concept you will soon be able to "see" its return. Just start giving love away and have faith that it will come back, someway, somehow, guaranteed.

So, why is it that we often feel like we are giving out love and not receiving it back? This can be for a few reasons including intention and recognition. If either of these is off, you may feel that love is passing you by. In the case of intention, it is important to know that giving love away in order to get certain results is not a good idea. If you are just trying to get a particular reaction from someone, this is called manipulation, not love. If your intention is to look altruistic in your giving, this is called being a good actor, not love. If your intention is to show others how good you are for giving love when others might not, this is called being a martyr, not love. If your intention is to make someone feel badly about not loving you even thought you love him or her, this is called being a victim, not love. The only way to give love is unconditionally. You should have no attachment to the outcome.

As for the concept of recognition, love often doesn't come back to us in the form that we want it. We don't even recognize that it has come back at all. We want it in a certain shape, height and color and look past all the other forms in which it might appear. If the man of our dreams isn't six feet tall with blue eyes and a fat wallet, then it's not right. Or, if our parents don't buy us a new car at graduation then they don't love us. Perhaps we expect our wife to know the exact golf clubs that we want for our birthday to prove that she loves us. Does your idea of love from your child mean that they always clean their room? Whatever measures we use to recognize love, there is a good chance we will have to change them.

Perhaps the man of our dreams is right in front of us and we don't recognize him because he appears in a different shape and size than we expected. Perhaps our parents love us tremendously, but they know that letting us earn the money to buy our own car will teach us greater lessons. Or our wife gets all dressed up and surprises us with a romantic candlelight dinner to show her love rather than buy us golf clubs. And those messy kids come home every night and give you a big hug and whisper "I love you" before putting their beautiful heads on the pillows you wish had been more properly plumped.

You tell me, is it possible that love has been arriving in packages slightly different than you expected and you overlooked it? Are you willing to let go of some of your expectations and look for love in the many shapes in which it may arrive? Life becomes a truly joyous experience when we recognize love in everyone and everything. It takes some practice and some shifts in perception, but life will become remarkable rewarding after you make this choice.

Once you start looking at love differently, you will no longer feel so attached to the old concept. As a matter of fact, you will begin experience love in so many ways that your love glass will seem full all the time. In this state of fullness you will feel even more generous and fulfilled. You won't depend on one person or one relationship to satisfy your needs. You will begin to remember unconditional love in all its goodness and abundance. Relax and enjoy love.

****

There is a deep well
Filled with a cool clear liquid
I drink from it and it sustains me
I offer it to others

They come to drink too
All who drink find peace
All who drink know love
Come join us at the endless well.

****

Love is patient, love is kind. It does not envy, it does not boast, it is not proud. It is not rude, it is not self-seeking, it is not easily angered, it keeps no records of wrongs. Love does not delight in evil but rejoices with the truth. It always protects, always trust, always hopes, always perseveres. I Corinthians 13:4-7

****

The infinite peace in knowing that you are loved eternally and that you are not judged but accepted just as you are a child of God a creation put on this earth to experience life but also to get closer to the truth the understanding the knowing of who and what we are one with God one with each other one with the world one with the universe true poetry in progress as a river flows so do we as one flowing rippling churning moving but always part of the river and it becomes more and more difficult to envision ourselves as separate from the whole for our drop would evaporate and disappear leaving the smallest trace of mineral deposit but hardly a true indication of what was once a drop of water choosing again to merge and journey in the way it was meant to with the knowing of the ultimate destination and the sense that it cannot be judged because it is all the same part of the whole moving splashing laughing at the rocks and swishing round the bends enjoying it all and never stopping to consider that it is anything but perfect in its being in its existence in its journey and in its love for that is what it is and that is what we are no more no less pure unconditional love

****

YOUR MUSTARD SEED MOMENT

When you wake up in the morning, look in the mirror and say to yourself, "I am loved." Look straight into your own eyes and say it out loud. "I am loved." Use it as a mantra. Repeat it to yourself over and over throughout the day. "I am loved. I am loved. I am loved. I am loved." Before you go to sleep at night say it to yourself. "I am loved. I am loved." If you keep repeating this for a few days, you will start believing it and you will find peace in this knowing. You are loved just the way you are.

Chapter 10

What Is Fear?

Fear is that feeling we get when we are unsure of the outcome of a particular situation. Or, if we do know what the outcome will be, we don't think we will be comfortable or happy with it. But what if we knew the ending and it guaranteed our happiness? That way, no matter how bad things seemed at the time, we knew that everything would turn out okay. For example, if you would video tape your favorite team and you knew already that they had won, you would not feel fearful while watching the video, even if they were losing for most of the game. If anything, you might actually be intrigued and excited to see how they pulled it off even when the odds were against them. You felt this way because you were sure of the outcome. You had faith that no matter how bad it looked, there would be a happy ending. We can practice the same faith in our lives everyday, but many of us don't.

Maybe we don't believe in that happy ending. Perhaps it seems too far away, or we believe that it happens to other people but not to us. Whatever our reasons, we are filled with fear and unhappiness. But the truth is that our happiness is guaranteed. We can live in heaven every day of our lives, but we have to make a choice. Do we continue to believe in our illusions or do we believe in the truth?

It is a vicious cycle and whichever way we turn, we are going to experience fear until we learn to let go. We feel fear because we believe in our illusion and we need to let our illusion go. We have an overwhelming fear of dying in all its forms and this includes the death of our old ways. But in order to survive, in order to live, we have to let our old ways die. Let go of the old habits, let go of the old thoughts, let go of the old judgments, let go of the old fears—just let go.

This is the part that frightens us most. Everything we know is tied up in those old beliefs, so what is left of us if we let go of all those things? The truth is left. The essence of who you really are is left. The part of you that really matters will survive. That is the miracle. From this death comes life–a resurrection. Our spirit will rise from the place we had it buried. Our old ways are like to stone before the tomb. We have piled it high and made it incredibly heavy. And worse yet, we've grown so attached to it. But move it away, roll the stone aside and experience the fullness of who you are. Experience the miracle. Experience the resurrection.

Perhaps you don't realize the value of that which lives inside the tomb. Perhaps you aren't sure of the wonder that waits within. Know that inside the tomb lives the glory of all that is, was and ever shall be. It is all truth, all love, all peace, all happiness, all beauty, all light. And the best part is that it is yours. It is everyone's. It is eternal and infinite. Claim this precious treasure now by rolling away the stone. Know a life that is complete and fulfilling. By letting go of fear we can enjoy every moment of every day and experience life and love like we've never experienced it before.

Many books have been written and pages have been filled with long explanations of our fears and how they hold us back. We meet people every day who have the same or similar fears, and somehow, being part of this group makes us more comfortable. But it is time to break away from the crowd. We don't need to be lulled into that false sense of security. Our fears keep us away from the things we are truly seeking. So let's not make this a group therapy session. Instead of dwelling on our fears, let's think of the wonders that await us once we let the fears go. Dwelling on the fears only brings more. We will now choose to dwell on love, on life and on miracles.

****

Our deepest fear is not that we are inadequate.
Our deepest fear is that we are powerful beyond measure.
It is our light, not our darkness, that most frightens us.
We ask ourselves, who am I to be brilliant,
gorgeous, talented and fabulous?
Actually, who are you not to be?
Your playing small doesn't serve the world.
There's nothing enlightened about shrinking so
that other people won't feel insecure around you.
We were born to make manifest the glory of God
that is within us.
It's not just in some of us, it's in everyone.
And as we let our light shine we unconsciously
give others permission to do the same.
As we are liberated from our own fears
our presence automatically liberates others.
-Nelson Mandela
Inaugural Speech 1994

Chapter 11

It's Your Choice

"To be or not to be, that is the question."
William Shakespeare

****

Every moment of every day you have a choice. You can choose to act out of love or out of fear. You can choose to make decisions of the ego or of God. You can choose to be in heaven or hell. You can choose chaos or peace. And, as Shakespeare wrote, you can choose to be or not to be. If you choose love, God, heaven and/or being, the world will seem like a much kinder place. But it does depend on you. The world may not change but your choice to see it differently can.

The reason this concept may rub us the wrong way is because it challenges us to take ownership of our situation. What choice did we make to lead us up to this place and what choice are we making to keep us there now? Do you like where you are? Then keep making the same choices. Are you unhappy with your life? Then start making different choices and start seeing the world differently. We are not victims of our circumstances, but we are victims of our choices. If we live our life each day with that truth we will probably begin to see things a little differently.

Some of you may be reading this saying "Yes, I want to make different choices because I don't like where I am, but how do I begin? How do I know which choice will serve me better than another? And, why do I keep making choices that take me someplace I don't want to be?" These are excellent questions. I have asked myself many of these questions too. We all need to begin with our intention. If our intention is to live life from a higher place, then we will see that some paths will be made clearer for us. Before we go any further, we need to get our intention straight. Then we can continue and with an open heart and an open mind we can listen for the stirring down deep that will help us to remember the truth.

When we make any decision, we either serve a greater good or we serve our ego (Edging God Out). Serving a greater good means we are making a love based decision. In serving our ego we make fear based decisions. The challenge is knowing which is which and also knowing that the ego will do everything in its power to keep us from getting too close to God. Once we remember our way home and find our oneness with the universe, there is no more need for the ego. It vanishes. In order to stay alive, the ego works devilishly hard to perpetuate our separateness. It makes our choices difficult by constantly showing us how an ego-based decision will serve us well. The ego does this out of the fear of its own death. Our goal then, if we want to be one with God is to stop listening to our ego and quiet ourselves to hear God.

If every new situation in our lives had clear markers leading us either to God or to ego, it would make life much easier. Right? Or would it? I'm not so sure. I have stood absolutely paralyzed at the most clearly marked junctures of my life. There was no doubt that one direction would bring happiness and the other direction disaster. And still I froze like a deer caught in headlights. Worse yet, there were numerous times when I insisted on moving down the path that warned of danger and steep inclines. I saw boulders teetering on either side of the road and the bridges were washed out too. But on I went, determined that I could survive this difficult and treacherous journey, only to find that it never lead me where I wanted to go. Now I know that I can be stubborn at times, but I also know that my ego played a big role in these choices.

However, once I began to see that my ego had its own agenda was I able to look past it and see that there was another way. And the minute I caught that glimpse, guess what happened? My ego went into over-drive to keep me confined to a life of chaos. It sent so many messages to me telling me that I didn't need to seek another path. It said I was strong enough to handle things on my own and I definitely didn't need a "crutch" like God. It took months of praying and meditating to see beyond my ego on a consistent basis. It didn't happen over night. After all, it took me many years to get to this place, and it was going to take work to get where I belonged. But work I did. I did not waiver in my faith that something better existed. You can do the same. It is your choice.

Many people will read this and point out that victims of disasters and child abuse do not make a choice to be in that place. Some may argue that even those souls made choices on a subconscious level to experience that pain. But even if you do not believe that, hopefully you can believe that those victims have a choice to look at their situation as a blessing or a curse. Helen Keller comes to mind when I think of someone who had to overcome tremendous disabilities. But look what she was able to accomplish because she chose to make a difference. She did not wallow in despair. She chose God over ego and love over fear. The list of people who had lived above and beyond their challenges is endless. Now it's our choice. Do you choose to be or not to be, that is the question.

****

Once upon a time in the Garden of Eden, all was one. All was beauty, all was peace, all was. But man began to believe himself as separate from the Divine, separate from beauty, separate from peace, separate from true self and true purpose. Man created his world, his illusion, his dream, so he could be in control. Or so he thought. He made the motions to act as God in a world that was a dream. But all the time, in his heart and his mind was a stirring, reminding him of the truth, the reality. He knew he was not truly in control, but his ego gave him no alternative. The ego coaxed him to build fences, to tame animals, to create a world that suited its needs. In the ego's world is need for right and wrong, black and white, war and peace, feast and famine, love and hate, truth and lies. The ego goads us into perpetuating our supposed separateness. How else would the ego survive unless it had its own "home" to live in? The ego needs the body–not the spirit. The ego needs illness–not the spirit. The ego needs catastrophe–not the spirit. The ego need to make us feel separate–not the spirit. And the ego doesn't want us to figure any of this out because then there wouldn't be any ego. There would only be spirit.

****

Dear Mother/Father,
I get it
I really get it
I've done this moment before
Many times before
Maybe it was a different town
Maybe the names have been changed to protect the innocent
But the point is that I did this before
And I didn't do it very well
So here I am
I have the opportunity to do this again
And this time I can do it better than before
Thank you for giving me the opportunity to choose again
Please guide my footsteps
Amen

****

Every day you have a choice
You can live life fully
Or you can live life small

Living small can often seem safe
Living small can often feel comfortable
But, living small will never seem fulfilling
For it does not serve the world
Have you ever wondered if this is it?
Have you ever wondered if this is all there is?
You ask these questions when you are living small
The good news is…
You can choose again
Choose to live passionately
Choose to live unconditionally
Choose to give soulfully
Choose to perceive nonjudgmentally
Choose to let go
The choice is yours
Or is it?

****

As a human being
Why do we make
The first word more important
Than the second?
It is obvious
That we have all become
Very good
At being human.

But now it's time
To be good at being
Stop for a second
And concentrate on being.

You have all the time
In the world
To be human
But it takes no time
To be.

****

YOUR MUSTARD SEED MOMENT

Choose to do something differently today. Anything. If you always drive the same way to work, choose a different route. If you always eat lunch at the same restaurant, choose a different restaurant. If you always wear sweats to bed, choose to wear something different (or nothing at all). If you always listen to the same radio station, choose another one. The point is to realize that you make choices every moment of every day. To be conscious of that will start you on the path to knowing the choices that will best serve you and the world.

Chapter 12

Please Take A Message

Coincidence is God's way of performing a miracle anonymously.
Anonymous

****

We talk about quieting the mind and being receptive to the messages of the universe. These messages are not new, it is just that we have forgotten many of them. When we learn to be still and listen to the voice in the wind or the whisper of a butterflies wings, when we take the time to plant a seed and watch it grow day by day, or we eat corn one precious kernel at a time, when we can take a step feeling our heels and toes touching the ground or we breathe slowly, filling our lungs gradually and fully expand, when we learn to do these things we will be able to know that the message is everywhere and in everything. If you can't do that yet, it's okay. Just know that it is there. And surely you will begin to notice. It will be as if a billboard was erected where once there was none or a mountain suddenly disappears from its place in the landscape. It will become that evident. Your intention to know it and your desire for the truth will bring the circumstances and people that will help you.

These truths or messages may come in the form of a coincidence or a miracle. Perhaps you will hear it in a child's laugh or in the words of a song. It may be in the next comic strip that you read or an advertisement for breakfast cereal. You will be amazed at the many ways you will be able to "hear" it. I've already mentioned that I find feathers whenever I am a little down and know that my angels are near to protect me. I also find coins on a daily basis and I recognize this as a way for the universe to remind me about abundance. You may find things that are very meaningful to you. Just know that nothing happens by accident, so if you feel you were meant to get a message, then you were.

Have fun with it. God has a tremendous sense of humor. One day when I really needed a pick-me-up, a big, fluffy, turquoise feather went tumbling by me on the ground. I couldn't help but laugh and feel better. Just the thought of a big blue angel flying around, or better yet, a white angel with a brightly colored boa wrapped around its neck had me in stitches. I felt better immediately.

Of course there are times when the messages are more serious too. But all in all, they always bring a smile to my face because they make me remember what I am a part of. And, just knowing that makes me happy.

****

Hear the message: Welcome, child. Welcome home. I welcome you although you have never left. It may feel like part of you died, but you have just begun to live. You thought you traveled a long path when in fact there was no path at all. You never really left. You remember now and that is why you are here. You made the journey as long and difficult as you wanted it to be. But now you are here. Welcome your brothers. Know that they are all a part of you. Feel the peace. You had the knowing and remembered your home. So, welcome. Welcome to your home.

****

Please show me the path
Please give me your hand
Please guide all my steps
Help me move when I stand.

I long for the journey
I am willing to go
But sometimes I'm scared
Of the things I don't know.

Just show me the path
And give me your hand
Please guide all my steps
Make me move when I stand.

****

Sometimes it comes as a wave. Sometimes it comes like a brick wall. Sometimes it seems to hide away, only to be found curled up in the most unlikely of places. But, all the time there is this knowing, this understanding that needs no explanation. It is just there and I feel a need to share it–share it with the world for all to hear. It is a message. It is a message of love, peace, compassion and faith.

Once you hear this message, you will see the world as you never have before. It will all seem clearer. And you will notice that the person standing in front of you will appear as your brother, the person to your right your sister, and the person to your left will appear as you–yes you. In reality they are all you. There is no difference, no delineation except for the ones you have created. Create no more. See no more boundaries, no more lines. The body is merely an illusion. Get beyond it and remember. Remember your oneness, your wholeness. Remember the love, the peace, the place where all is. Remember the Divine, the all-knowing, the all-seeing, the everything-that-is-and-is-not. Quiet your self. Quiet your mind. Go in. Go in more. Go to that place where all is quiet, all is peace, all is and no thing is. Meditate in that place and know. Go there now.

****

Share your peace
Share your love
Give it generously and unconditionally
Unto the world
You are now here
Go with enthusiasm
Go with love
Let them see it in your face
Let them hear it in your voice
Let them experience it in your walk
Be gentle but firm
Be at peace
You are ready

****

Marvel at God's handiwork
Every day
Every where
The first crocus peeking through the snow in Spring
The smell of the air after a hard Summer rain
Scampering squirrels hording acorns in Autumn
The beautiful silence of a gentle Winter snow
I draw a deep breath at the touch of a hand
I smile at the laugh of a child
I see God's handiwork
Every day
Every where.

****

How often have you said that you asked God a question but you didn't get an answer? No booming voice came from the sky, and no little angel sat on you shoulder and whispered in your ear. The answer just didn't come to you. But, were you really listening?

I believe that God speaks through everything and everyone. So, I've learned to treat each word and sentence someone speaks to me as if it is a precious gem from God. I wouldn't want to miss that diamond in the rough just because it didn't look like anything on the outside. I listen intently, letting each thought register in my mind and in my heart, always knowing that there is a message in there somewhere. Now, I don't know if this message is meant for me to use now or later, so I don't make judgments as to its value. I simply know that God wanted me to hear it. That is why this person is speaking to me right now, at this moment. By interrupting or cutting the speaker short I am saying that I believe what I have on my mind is more important than what he or she is saying to me. In so doing I miss out on the most valuable treasure. I miss a precious gem from God because I am too busy with my own thoughts. I have often been pleasantly surprised that the conversation which seemed to have the least value to me at the moment was something I needed later.

This takes practice. Don't be discouraged if it doesn't come easily. We have been conditioned to think that having a great conversation means knowing the right thing to say. Meanwhile, the secret is knowing the right thing to hear.

****

Dear Angels,
I can't seem to find peace.
Why?

Dear Child,
Oh little lamb

We cry when you cry
We hurt when you hurt
We don't want you to feel pain
You will always find the peace you seek
When you put your trust in the Beloved
He doesn't want you to feel pain
She wants you to know peace
But you can't find it
If you live with expectations
Trust that the Beloved has a plan
Have faith that everything happens for a reason
And in that faith and trust you will find peace
Come dance with us, child
Come sing a song
And know you are loved.

****

YOUR MUSTARD SEED MOMENT

Be conscious of every "coincidence" that happens in your life. Write them down. It is not necessary to find a deep meaning in each one, but take note. Did the person you were just thinking about call you? Did the song you were humming in your head start playing on the radio? Did you pick up a book and the first sentence explains exactly how you were feeling at the moment? Just keep track. You will be amazed at how any more you will notice once you are conscious of them.

Chapter 13

Why Are We Here?

Why is it easier to jump out of bed early in the morning of the day you are leaving on vacation than on a day when you just have a few errands to run? Why is it easier to prepare a beautiful meal for a dear friend than it is to get off the couch and throw a waffle in the toaster for yourself? Why is it easier to get to the bank on payday than it is to get to the post office to buy stamps for your bills? One is not more important than the other. Both give us desired results. But with one we feel more motivation, a sense of inspiration, a sense of purpose.

I have often heard the example used that most people would not walk a tightrope between two skyscrapers. But if we knew a loved one was in the opposite building and their life depended on us getting across, somehow a lot of people in this world would learn how to walk a tightrope. It would be too important not to.

Let's stick with this visualization for a moment, only this time there is no one in the other building. However, the building that you are standing on is burning. The flames are beginning to lick at your feet and it is getting very uncomfortable. The life you are going to save by crossing the tightrope is your own. It just takes the faith and courage needed to make the first step, followed by the second and third. The choice is to live or die. And it gets better. If you cross the tightrope you will not only live, you will actually experience eternal life, along with happiness, love, peace, abundance. You will have everything your soul desires. What greater reason than to cross the tightrope? And still most of us would stand immobilized by our fear of the unknown, the fear of letting go. It is the fear of leaving what we already know, even if it is burning down around us.

The only way to overcome this is to have a sense of purpose that is greater than our fear. Once we determine that purpose our vision begins to clear. The fears melt away because they no longer serve us. We no longer choose to be bound by our old ways of thinking. We choose again. We live again.

On the burning building we leave behind our old body, our old thoughts, our old habits. With each step on the tightrope we become rejuvenated in body, mind and soul. And with each step towards the other building we will find that the distance diminishes by an amount greater than our step. Our inch of faith will be multiplied ten-fold. What seemed like miles of thin terrifying wire begins to look more like yards of wide cable. And with a few more steps, the yards become feet and the cable becomes a steel girder. Before you know it, you walk or even fly the last few inches over a thick plush carpet.

But you can't see this from your place on the burning building. You have heard some stories, but there was no way to know for sure what awaited you on the other side of the tightrope. And the voices scream for you to stay behind, to stay where you are. They mean well, but it is their fears that are speaking. You move forward, separating yourself from the crowd and your light becomes brighter. People will see that light and know that it is good. Your light will serve as a beacon for others to follow. The path will be a little clearer for your passing, and the more that pass over to the other building, the more illuminated the path becomes. I thank God regularly for those who had the courage and faith to pass before me making my trip that much easier. And it is my hope that my step will make it a bit easier for others to cross. That is my purpose.

And what is your purpose? No one can answer for you. That is part of your journey, to determine what will move you beyond your fears. If just the knowledge that you can move out of discomfort and into bliss is not enough, then search your heart. Be quiet with it. Listen to the song of your soul. With faith the size of a mustard seed you will be able to remember your purpose and change your life. Give yourself that chance.

Every morning, before I leave my home, I read an excerpt from A Course in Miracle to remind me for the purpose I have found in my life. I keep it on the wall by the door so I can read it as often as possible. It goes like this:

I am here only to be truly helpful.

I am here to represent Him who sent me.

I do not have to worry about what to say or what to do because He who sent me will direct me.

I am content to be wherever He wishes, knowing He goes there with me.

I will be healed as I let Him teach me to heal.

This helps to keep me focused on my purpose each day. I love to help others. I get a sense of joy and fulfillment from it. The desire to be truly helpful is a purpose that helps me to overcome any fears. On those days when I am less than enthusiastic to walk out the door, I read this and leave with new confidence.

A desire to help others has another benefit. By focusing my attention on others I take my focus off myself. I don't dwell as much on my aches and pains, or my latest dilemma. I instead put my energy into assisting others and my "troubles" fade into the background. It is amazing how a headache that was distracting you while you were sitting at home suddenly vanishes while you are out and about doing your part to make the world better. It's a wonderful remedy for many of the things that ail you.

Finding your purpose can take some time. Remember how long it took you to choose a major in college? Or what house to buy, which job to take, where to live? But, it is well worth your attention. What do you like to do? What are you really good at? Does anything strike a chord? If not, try meditating on it. If that still doesn't work, it's okay. But don't stand still while you are trying to figure it out. The answer may be waiting for you right outside your door. Get out. Do things. Interact with people. And always remember what waits for you on the other building. It's just a few steps away.

****

Dear God,
Please use me as a living example
Of your love and peace.
I can think of no more fulfilling life
Than a life lived in the glory of you.
Amen

****

Dear God,
Please let your light shine through me.
Let me be an example of your unconditional love.
Let me bring hope to others
With smiles and laughter.
Guide my words and my steps.
Let me serve your greater purpose.
Amen

****

I have a recurring vision. I am standing behind a white picket fence. The fence is only about three feet high and the slats are spaced far enough apart that you can easily see through them. Now, typically a fence would surround a house or a yard, but this fence is in a field of golden grass. The field is edged on the side closest to the fence by a thick and deep forest. It is dark in the forest because the light cannot penetrate the densely over-hanging trees. This darkness is in distinct contrast to the sunshine of the field. I am clothed in a flowing dress with pastel colors resembling a water-color painting, as if someone had taken a large paintbrush to paint it. It is sleeveless and the hem of the dress touches my bare feet. In my arms is a child, about two years of age. The child is balanced on my hip and I hold it closely. It is a beautiful child with dark skin, shiny dark hair and bright brown eyes. There is a gate where we stand behind the fence.. The gate is open and people are coming out of the forest and walking through the gate to the field. We touch and greet each person as they walk by and we all seem to know each other. There is great peace in this passage.

****

Dear God,
Please let each person I meet today
Experience the joy and peace that radiates from you.
Please let them feel the peace which fills my heart.
And unconditional love
Please guide my steps so I may serve you
As completely as possible
Thank you for your love.
Amen

****

What does it mean to be a child of God?
It means that we have an obligation to serve a greater good.
It means that all living creatures are our brothers and sisters.
It means that we all share one Creator and thus there is unity amongst all of us.
It means that we deserve the best of everything this world has to offer.
It means that we need to give back our best just as easily.
It means that no life is meaningless and we need to treat it as precious.

It means that we need to practice unconditional love and learn not to judge each other.

It means that God already gave his Son for the forgiveness of all our sins, so we don't need to crucify ourselves any more.

It means that we are loved thoroughly and completely and we should never forget that.

It means that we are never alone.

It means that once we "get it" we can help others to "get it" too.

It means that we can find peace when our lives are chaotic.

It means that we must see ourselves as one.

It means that we are related to the Divine so how can we go wrong?

****

YOUR MUSTARD SEED MOMENT

Take some time to think about your purpose. What are your talents? What do you love to do? What do you do really well? What do you get great joy from? These may be hints as to where your purpose lies. Once you get a feel for what your purpose may be, start to think about how you can use it to serve a greater good. The options are endless, but think what an incredible world it will be when everyone uses their time, energy and talents to do something truly fulfilling. Wow.

Chapter 14

Where We Are One

Namaste–The place in me that is one with the universe honors the place in you that is one with the universe and when we are both in that place we are one with all creation.

****

There is a beautiful, sacred place that is exactly the same in each of us. It is the place where peace and unconditional love exist, where differences are irrelevant and we know we are one. For some of us it is an easy place to find, for others it seems hidden. But know that it does exist in everyone. When we acknowledge and honor this place in each other, we acknowledge and honor our oneness.

When living from that oneness we experience a wholeness that extends outward. It extends to friends, family, and even strangers. It also extends out into the environment. Nothing and no one stands apart from this oneness. Our differences melt away in the glory of this place.

Our greatest obstacle to seeing this as truth is our egos. Our egos put blinders on us making it more difficult to recognize a total stranger as our brother. Our egos believe in separation. Our egos believe in difference. And our egos want to keep it that way. But, we have the ability to work around it if we choose to. We have to remember where we are one. If we want to get past the ego we need to go to our higher source.

Learning to be humble helps when remembering our oneness. If we are arrogant and ego-driven we are trying to prove that we are better than someone else. There is no room for that in oneness. Where we are one, we are equally wonderful and wonderfully equal. There is no one who is better than another. This works in reverse too. Being humble does not mean that we can be worse than anyone either. Shrinking does not serve us, or the world. It can be as frustrating and unattractive as being arrogant. In order to be all we can be, we need to move away from that way of thinking. We were all made perfect and perfect we are. We can't be better than or worse than anyone because we are all God's children, which makes us all perfect. Period.

Recognizing this perfection also allows us to stop judging. We would stop judging ourselves as well as others. Can you just imagine a world in which no one is called fat or skinny, tall or short, black or white, old or young? There would be no categories or compartments, no need to classify each other. Everyone would be on a level playing field. That is the way we would view the world through enlightened eyes, because none of the supposed difference would matter.

Seeing our oneness is a wonderful thing. It also brings with it a sense of responsibility. Once we realize that we are all connected, we also realize that everything we do to ourselves effects everyone else. If we smoke, everyone has the potential for lung ailments. If we smile, everyone feels happy. If we eat junk food, everyone feels lethargic. If we exercise, everyone reaps the benefits. Our habits affect everyone whether we do them behind closed doors or in public. If you are hurting yourself, you are hurting everyone. The place where we are one is affected. We also have a responsibility to our environment. Remember, there is a place where we are one with everything and this includes the earth. Mistreat the world and we mistreat ourselves. Disrespect of the environment or a fellow living creature affects us all, no matter how small an infraction it is. We need to practice respecting our fellow humans, our world, and ourselves if we are to achieve a higher level of understanding. In essence, we have to stop littering our universe on all levels. Let's remember our oneness by letting go of our ego, being humble, practicing non-judgment and seeing ourselves as part of the universal consciousness.

****

As I walked across the field tonight
I could see my shadow directly in front of me
I turned around to see the moon, full and bright
It was giving out so much light
I felt as if I could walk on the beams
I became lighter somehow
As if I could float
I thought of flying
And it was beautiful
The moon changed me tonight
And I changed the moon

****

Let's end the differences
Let's end the illusions
In reality there are no differences
There is oneness
Let's experience our atonement
At-one-ment
There is a place in you
That is the same as the place in me
And when we are both in that place
We are one
Honor that place
Honor the oneness

****

Wake from the dream
Wake from the illusion
Let go of the grip
And break free of ego's mad hold

****

Dear God,
Please let me recognize myself in my brothers
And my brothers in myself
If we could all learn to do this
With every person we meet
Every day, every where
There would be no conflict
There would be no pain
Because hurting my brother
Is hurting myself
Please let me see the beauty
And the innocence in my brother
And in myself
Amen

****

Our healing begins
When we can see
That there are no differences
There are no boundaries
There are no limits
We are one

And we are whole
Let's begin the healing
Let's begin the at-one-ment

****

We are so in love
With "who we are"
We are a tall, handsome doctor
We are a short, divorced mother
A happy musician
An educated professor
But is this really who we are?
How can it be if it can change
In a heartbeat?
What we really are is spirit
Dancing through life
In beautiful costumes
With beautiful stories
Intricate and well acted
But never confuse the character we play
With the spirit that we are.

****

YOUR MUSTARD SEED MOMENT

Just for one day, practice nonjudgment. Every time a judgmental thought goes through your head, stop. Tell yourself that you will ponder it more tomorrow, but not today. Today there will be no judging. No one is right. No one is wrong. There is no good. There is no bad. Just don't judge for one whole day. It will change the way you see the world.

Chapter 15

Relationships

Relationships allow us to practice our oneness. It is all fine and good if we sit alone in a room and say that we love everyone and everything. But what happens if we walk past our neighbor and don't say hello. Or maybe we cut someone off as we get on the highway. Perhaps we get short with the person who gives us the wrong order at the restaurant. All of these are relationships and they all give us the opportunity to be loving, forgiving, and neighborly. It also gives us the opportunity to see where we are one with everyone else. Relationships allow us to see our unity.

So what about romantic relationships? If you are looking for that special relationship to make you happy, secure, loved, and cared for you are going to run into trouble. We have been fairy-taled to death thinking that knights in shining armor rescue damsels in distress and ride off into the sunset to live happily ever after. But this is not reality. The feeling of love, warmth, happiness and security starts with you. Be your own knight. Rescue yourself. Don't wait for some "perfect" person to come and do it for you.

Some of you may be saying, "I'm not looking for a perfect person. I'm willing to compromise." That is wonderful, but you still need to take a close look at what you <u>are</u> looking for. I agree that compromise is a powerful and necessary component in any relationship. However, are you compromising on issues that go against your best judgments just because it is more important to be in a relationship than to be alone? Are you trying to fit that "non-perfect" person into your life just for the sake of having someone there? Ask yourself why it is so difficult to be alone. There is a good chance that if you don't enjoy your own company, others won't enjoy it either.

This brings up another point. So many people have created a list of attributes they would like to find in their future mate. What are the attributes your future mate will look for in you? Working on your own personal list is far more important than worrying about what Mr. or Ms. Wonderful will be like. If you do your work, the right person will come along at the right time. You can count on it.

Relationships aren't only for romantic reasons. As a matter of fact, relationships are not just with people. They can be with anything. You name it and you are having a relationship with it. You are having a relationship with your car, your house, your clothes, and this book. If this sounds strange to you it is because you are focusing on the romantic aspect of relationships. Meanwhile, these everyday, everything relationships are just as important, if not more so, than any romantic relationship. How you treat even inanimate objects can be very telling of how you treat other things in your life. Start by appreciating and respecting all relationships and your people relationships will get better.

The relationships that you need to get straight first are those with yourself and with God. Develop these. Learn to love yourself and God before you tackle the world. Enjoy your ALONE time. Get to know yourself and get reacquainted with God. These two relationships by themselves can be tremendously fulfilling. Get these straight and the rest will fall into place. And, if you learn to rely on yourself and God you will be less needy in your other relationships.

Have you ever met someone who just seems to have it all together? They seem to know where they are going and what they are doing. They emanate a sense of peace and confidence and you can't help but want to be around them. They make you feel good just by spending time with them. In a short time you feel comfortable in their presence and you might even find yourself telling them things you don't normally share with others. This is probably because you can sense that they don't have an agenda. They are comfortable with who and what they are. They have made peace with themselves and their maker and it reflects back out into the world from their very being. We can all develop that feeling. We can become our own best friend and allow a higher source to guide us. But watch out. When this happens you will hardly believe all of the wonderful relationships that will come into you life. Do your part and the world will respond.

****

Dear God,
I trust in your plan
I know that each of us is on a specific path
But it is hard to see someone I care about suffer
Please help me to know how much to do
And help me know how much to say
Please guide my words and my actions
Let me know when I should leave it alone
I want so much to be truly helpful
But I don't always know how
I know that if I keep my heart open
Your message will be clear to me
Amen

****

I want to scream and yell and stamp my feet
I have worked so hard to find balance and peace
I am more centered now
And I see life from a more beautiful place
So, why all the drama?
Why is there someone in my life turning it all upside down?

How do I keep my boat from tipping on such stormy seas?
How do I stay centered?
I want to scream
I am so angry
I feel out of control
I need help
Dear God, please help
Help me to see this differently
Help me to know unconditional love
Help me to find forgiveness
I know it is not my place to judge
I know it is not my place to be in control
I give the reins to you
Please help me to find a way to see through this
And, please help me find my peace again.

****

The end of a relationship can be so painful
No matter how many times you tell yourself it will be for the best
It still hurts
I need to find peace at a moment when I feel turmoil
I want to get through this experience as a stronger person.
I feel like I just want to sleep for days and not talk to anyone
I hurt
Dear God, please ease my pain
Please show me the way to happiness again
Allow me to see the night as not so dark
And the sun just a little brighter
I ask you to fill my broken heart with your love and peace

****

Dear God,
I hand all my relationships to you
Please take them and use them
For your greater good
My view is so small
I cannot possibly see the larger purpose
But I trust in you
Please show me the way.
Amen

****

Dear God,
WHY?
Please help me see this differently
I hurt a lot
And I don't understand
I thought this was different
How can I be so wrong?
Please help me.
Amen

****

Two souls come together
We know there is work to be done
But first we need to establish trust
A foundation must be built
Before we expose our wounds
Or express our vulnerabilities
Remember, your partner is not your crutch
Or someone to lift you every time you are down

Your partner is there to love you
And walk beside you along the journey
Your relationship is a holy ground
Not a dumping ground
So, treat it with tenderness and respect
Listen attentively
Look adoringly
Touch tenderly
Smile genuinely
Laugh loudly
Enjoy greatly
Praise often
When the work of your souls becomes apparent
You will both come from a better place
A place of comfort, strength, trust and peace
And then, only then, can the real work begin

****

YOUR MUSTARD SEED MOMENT

Make a date with yourself. Go to a nice restaurant, see a movie, go to a museum, take a walk in the woods or along the beach. Enjoy your own company. Develop a loving relationship with yourself before you worry about your relationship with anyone or anything else. Get to really like yourself. If you have some areas about yourself that you are not happy with, find a self-help book or an audiotape that deals with that subject. You will be amazed at the change in all of your relationships once you get your relationship with yourself healthy.

Chapter 16

Now Here

So, where does this all leave us? It leaves us nowhere. That's right. After all that work we are left NOW-HERE, the only place and time that really exists. We have all spent minutes, hours, even days worrying about the future or fretting over the past. Meanwhile we are missing the precious NowHere. We can't change the past and we can't predict the future, but we can enjoy this moment. We can make a choice right now to enjoy right now. Don't let another second go by without appreciating exactly where you are now.

If there is just one message you can take from this book it should be: relax and enjoy NowHere. Let go of space/time and all the limitations it brings. Try not wearing a watch for a day or two. Go on vacation without a pager or cell phone. Hide your appointment book for a few days. Plan a few days to just live. Take a walk in the woods. Sleep late. Have an impromptu picnic. Catch a matinee. Take a long drive. Eat at a new restaurant. Buy a cookbook, pick a recipe and cook away. Buy some water-colors, brushes, paper and paint. Start and finish a crossword puzzle. Sing really loud to the radio. Go to a museum. Take a bath with lots of bubbles and candlelight. Listen to some soothing music. Write a poem. Read a book. Make a hopscotch board and play hopscotch. Send a card to a friend. Go to a park and feed the birds. See a play. Fly a kite. Build a snow-man. Take a walk on the beach. Say hello to a stranger. Celebrate life.

Pick a life celebrating-activity and stick to it. Keep a journal of what you did and how it made you feel. You will find that you even begin to enjoy your more mundane tasks because of these activities. You will be able to see the beauty of the suds in a sink full of dirty dishes or the way raindrops fall on the windshield of your car. A kernel of popcorn will suddenly look very interesting and smell even more delicious. Then feel how it melts on your tongue or hear the crunch when you bite it. Doesn't it taste wonderful? Eat a bowl of popcorn one kernel at a time and appreciate each one as if it is you first and last.

When I talk about these exercises of mindfulness, people say it takes a lot of thought, and they feel it is too much work. Well, the news is that you were thinking while you were eating your bowl of popcorn anyway. At least this way you are thinking about what you are doing right at the moment. You are enjoying NowHere. You aren't wondering what will happen later or what would have happened if you did something differently before. You are NowHere and mindful of it. Try it. It can be very enlightening.

Did you ever notice that worrying about something doesn't help? That's because there are only two types of events in you life. There are events you can do something about and the ones you can do nothing about. If the event is one in which you can participate, then do so. Don't worry about it, just do something. The other events are out of your control. So stop worrying about them. They are going to happen whether or not you worry. Don't make an art form out of worrying, It takes you away from NowHere and sucks the life out of you. It's not worth it.

It is truly your choice, every moment of every day to enjoy the moment or not. You can choose to live NowHere or somewhere else and your life will change if you pick NowHere. Don't wait another second. Don't waste another moment. Relax, take a deep breath and choose to love yourself and love this very moment. We are not guaranteed tomorrow or even an hour from now. But we do have NowHere. Enjoy it and be at peace!

****

It's time to put it all to the test

It's time to set the goals
It's time to name the day
It's time to make it happen
It's time to take action and move
It's time to apply the principals
It's time to believe
It's time to trust
It's time to do
It's time to continue learning
It's time to meet people
It's time to pray harder
It's time to use our strengths
It's time to dream
It's time to accomplish the dream
It's time to be alive
It's time to dance
It's time to love
It's time to be loved
It's time to know that we can
It's time to live life to the fullest
It's time to breathe deep…deeper
It's time to reap
It's time to sow
It's time to give
It's time to be
It's time to be
It's time to be

****

To know now is to now know
That now is all

You now know the secret
That is it
That is all
Now is all

****

To experience this moment
To love this moment
To know this moment
To be in this moment
To find peace in this moment
To feel joy in this moment
To give in this moment
To breathe this moment
To live this moment
To hear this moment
Stop for this moment
And be in this moment

****

YOUR MUSTARD SEED MOMENT

Practice mindfulness. Choose an activity and really concentrate on what you are doing. For example, if you are washing the dishes, spend that time thinking about what you are doing. Watch the water as it fills the sink. Look at the different colors that are reflected in the bubbles. Feel the sponge fill with water. Touch each pot, pan, dish and glass as if it is made of gold. Enjoy the experience. Be in that moment. Be NowHere.

Afterword

What good is a book if after reading it you simply place it on a shelf to become part of a pretty collection? It's like eating a meal that looks good, smells good and tastes good, but it doesn't give you any nutrition. You can eat and eat, meal after meal, but if your body doesn't absorb the necessary vitamins and minerals you will starve to death.

Reading books without properly digesting the information can bring the same unfortunate results. We fill ourselves up with good information but don't take the time to incorporate any of it into our lives. It can take a bit of conscious effort, but if you already took the time to pick up this book it is worth a few extra moments to take one of the ideas you have read and make it your own. At the end of each chapter is a simple exercise meant to help you on your journey. Take a leap of faith and try at least one of them, if not all of them.

Remember, it is no coincidence that you have picked up this book and are reading this page. Now find out what it is that you are meant to take from it. It's your choice. You can treat it like another bag of empty calories or you can savor it like a seven course meal (with mustard on the side.)